## Also by Miguel Algarín

*Action: The Nuyorican Poets Cafe Theater Festival*

*Aloud: The Nuyorican Poets Cafe Anthology*

*Time's Now/Ya Es Tiempo*

*Body Bee Callin From the Twenty-First Century*

*On Call*

*Mongo Affair*

*Song of Protest*
    by Pablo Neruda, translated by Miguel Algarín

*Nuyorican Poetry: An Anthology of New York Puerto Rican Words and Feelings*

# LOVE IS HARD WORK

## MEMORIAS DE LOISAIDA

## MIGUEL ALGARÍN

SCRIBNER POETRY

SCRIBNER POETRY
Simon & Schuster Inc.
Rockefeller Center
1230 Avenue of the Americas
New York, NY 10020

SCRIBNER POETRY and design are
trademarks of Simon & Schuster Inc.

*Designed by Brooke Zimmer*
*Set in Bembo*

Manufactured in the United States of America

10 9 8 7 6 5 4 3 2 1

Library of Congress Cataloging-in-Publication Data
Algarín, Miguel.
    Love is hard work / Miguel Algarín.
            p.   cm.
    I. Title.
PS3551.L359L6    1997

811'.54—dc21    97-2093
CIP

ISBN 0-684-82517-1

**To Richard August**

## Acknowledgments

I would like to thank Loisaida, the Nuyorican Poets Cafe, and the rich and varied city of New York.

# CONTENTS

# Introduction

*The Minister of Loisaida*
by Ishmael Reed

The immensely huggable Miguel Algarín has a big heart. That would be enough, but the genius of Miguel Algarín is that he's able to get his generosity of spirit down on paper. This is our good fortune.

Whether he's writing about Angels, one-winged, benevolent or aggressive, or about plagues that are devastating the inner cities, barrios and artistic communities, Algarín's pen is fluid, fecund, many-tongued, powerful, moving and exciting.

The language is fabulous, but Miguel does not see language as an end in itself, the obsession of the cold-blooded school of modern poetry. The poetry is as sophisticated as the author, who is capable of leading a theater audience in a discussion of the links between William Shakespeare and Adrienne Kennedy and of ordering in French at a New Orleans restaurant. He is a professor who nevertheless hasn't lost the common touch. Some of these poems are three-hankie poems. They are about the love of Miguel's life: The People. He moves through the city with a receptive consciousness. He believes with García Lorca that the poet is the professor of the five senses, so he savors each day as though it were a large spicy meal. Homemade jams. We not only see the scenes that Miguel paints in these poems, but we get the odors, the tastes, the music and the colors.

But tragedy is just as much a part of life as enjoyment, and Algarín chronicles the transition of his friends and loved ones from this life to another. Algarín records the Festival of the Living as well as the Festival of the Dead.

During the 1960s, an alliance of black and Puerto Rican writers energized the arts of the Lower East Side, only to have a journalist from the *Herald Tribune* ethnically white out the scene in an article that mentioned only one African-American writer.

Many of those black and Puerto Rican writers have dispersed, but Miguel Algarín is one of those who remained. He kept the spirit of the sixties going and became the godfather of several generations of artists and writers who have arrived on the scene since then. He is the minister, part-time mayor and full-time poet laureate of the Loisaida, that community of poetic souls which reaches from New York to Osaka, Amsterdam, Jo'Burg and London, Manila and Havana.

# I

# NUYORICAN ANGELS

# P R O E M

## i

Angels are human interactions with the incorporeal world. Sometimes it seems as if the angel is an object outside the body that is transforming internal time and space into a metaphysical thunderstorm. However, more often it is the possession of the body by biological changes in pulse rate, blood pressure and oxygen levels that can make you levitate internally, while the state of mind possessing you whips your limbs and innards into a frenzy. Angels are sometimes people, objects or simply live-wire ideas. The connection with this world of direct electricity can be controlled in part by letting go of the self in order to let the typhoon through, tidying up internal space afterwards.

# NUYORICAN ANGEL

Lines of fluid fire
shoot from the index finger
of the first angel,
his eyes penetrate emotional lead,
parting flesh woven time.
No, this Angel is not soft light—
he moves in compulsive, phlegmatic,
thick, muscular thrusts,
he enters pulsating,
kicking the mind apart,
rousing violent torrents
of liberating, sensual blood flows.
Swift, anxious yearning
fuels his desire to enter
the temple of live bodies,
no membrane can stop
his arrogant parting of the skin,
he scorches living flesh.

# NUYORICAN ANGEL OF IMPLOSION

The ceiling lowered
the floor and walls crumbled,
the news crumpled internal space,
breathing near-stopped,
the news traveled downstream
the mind rejected radio-wave-telephone-wire
information, no entrance, no recognition,
this is not happening,
this trip will not be changed,
this city will not be bombed,
take it back,
what was said has not been heard.
He hung up the phone distracted,
no tears flushed his despair,
he held on tight to let the seconds pass.
The backdraft caused by the Angel's wing
Saran-wrapped his mouth and nose—
resuscitation started
after inner body building collapsed.

# NUYORICAN ANGEL HELEN

98.5 percent closed colon,
it's a wonder how she's eaten
these last ten weeks.
Helen seems ready,
she opens her eyes to empty space,
not much emotion
when dying's the action,
it's the other side of the flatline,
right over the creek into heaven.

# NUYORICAN ANGEL ON MAUNDY THURSDAY

## (The Passing On of Tradition)

*(For Savion Glover and Gregory Hines)*

Savion's feet are swollen,
his heart pounds violently,
he stands, holding a bowl filled with purified water,
no point in pressing the empty air,
it wouldn't register,
better he should wash Gregory's feet
and then clean the sweat off of
every tap dancer that has ever beat the floor
catching each bead of sweat
that drops a kick ahead of the rhythm.
Savion, towel and bowl of water in hand,
approaches Gregory—
"What do you think? I don't dance
like this by myself," says Gregory to Savion,
as he offers his feet for the washing.

# TRANSPARENT NUYORICAN ANGEL

Mitch looks into the coffin,
sees himself,
turns his sight around the room,
spots a mirror,
squares himself cara a cara
with the image reflector
and sees a Van Gogh
*Sunflowers* reproduction
hanging on a maroon-colored
wallboard,
the rocking chair just beneath
the sunflowers in full bloom,
the cut, dried red carnations placed
on the rickety coffee table,
Mitch sees all except himself.

# NUYORICAN ONE WING
## OLIVE-SKINNED ANGEL

He came at Mitch late in his sleep,
there was no stirring of the air,
one wing does not stir up earthly air,
thus his movement avoids
whipping up sandstorms and wind torrents.
He wore sandals with long leather strips,
he had a tattoo of a Nubian boy
at the top of his right calf, behind the knee.
His long black hair covered his olive skin.
He began to spin on his right leg
and as he turned, leaves, twigs, herbs,
shot out, dropped and grew in his hair.
He said, "Harvest these balms from my body,
drink, eat, cure your wounds
and give thanks for what grows on me."
Mitch trembled with desire and need,
yet to touch the olive-skinned Angel seemed too selfish.

# OBESE NUYORICAN ANGEL

"Hold on to very little,
the more you keep, the weightier the tub
of lard that houses your ego."
Mitch drew the candle close,
snuffed it,
insults bind themselves to fat
tighter than calories,
so he turned the mirrors,
all reflections of self vanished.
"Don't forget your body is a compost heap
of stewed carrion
and dead leaves."
He emptied his mind of vanity
and entered the cupboard of grease
the rebel angel had just nailed him to.

# NUYORICAN ANGEL
# OF FORGETFULNESS

At the end of his visit,
he took away my memory of it.

# NUYORICAN ANGEL VOICE

*(For Little Jimmy Scott)*

Little Jimmy Scott speaks music,
stringing his lyrics together,
never has any angel heard him sing a melody,
*"All of me,*
*why not take all of me."*
Jimmy talks his passion by hitting the syllables
the joy of sweat on limbs becoming one blood flow
*"That's deeper than the deep blue sea is,"*
you see
*"that's how deep it goes if it's real*
*but if you let me love you*
*it's for sure I'm gonna love you*
*all the way."*
Never a melody,
always hitting the feeling,
androgyny never existed except in someone's body,
if it's a question of *"all the way,*
*only a fool can say,"*
without being loved all the way,
yes! *"all the way,"*
'til *"day by day"* we make it deeper by far
than any ocean,
I am wider than your hold can take,
but I'm yours to stay
through the years
*"day by day"*
you're making all my dreams come true,
all the way to where I am yours alone
yes, I am yours to stay,
'til you understand how much I love you

and those mourning roses
I've sprinkled with tears,
how I've traveled to be where you are,
how long is the journey from here to your star
and if I ever lose you
how much would I cry
*"just how deep is the ocean*
*how high is the sky,"*
just how long is the suffering
yes, *"how deep is the ocean,*
*how high is the sky,"*
before seeing you gets hazy
and a gentle touch turns hard.

# MAYAN NUYORICAN ANGEL

Radio signals sent to the satellite bird
spread briskly played mambo beats from
the south east corner of Tompkins Square Park
right into Tokyo at 1 a.m.
"what's it all about Akira?"
our Lower East Side English radio-speak
sounds like Mayan to the Japanese,
and as to the Mayan
it is probably true that the 1990s Nuyoricans
mix shoyu and wasabi as they please,
and it is absolutely true that Nuyoricans
order Moriawase with their pasteles
and that the Itamae-San
serves his sushi creations in perfect harmony
with alcapurrias and beef patties,
over blue corn tortillas.

# NUYORICAN ANGEL SHE-CRABS

Traveled over land to Portland,
you can call it a rapid transit orgasm,
you can call it beans over crab cakes
two blocks away from the Portland Hilton,
you can call it sexual harassment of she-crabs,
you can call it palming belly buttons in September.

# NUYORICAN ANGEL CHARLENE

I heard fist bones on flesh,
the pounding, the hammering
of spandex covered ribs,
the beater and the beaten!
A white man approaches,
the beating continues,
a black man comes near,
the blows rain unabated,
a policeman looks away.
"No one notices violence anymore," says a Latino
as he counts the slaps, punches and kicks.
There is no angel to interfere,
to deliver broken-wing Charlene
from her gruesome mauling.

# NUYORICAN ANGEL OF RECORDS

*(For Miguel Piñero)*

Philosophy met her brother Time
and went for a walk,
when they reached Truth's house,
Lies, Greed and Envy
were visiting
but it took History
to point out to Time
that Truth didn't have her house
in order,
in fact,
she was so lineally sloppy
that History refused
to tell time in her house,
Lies, Greed and Envy
laughed till they urinated Pain
which caused a thunderstorm
of maladies known as Plagues.

# JAPANESE NUYORICAN ANGEL

## ("I Don't Want to Busy My Desires")

No, I don't want to busy my desires,
I'll just hold a stone
to feel an embrace,
too much of anything
is not happiness.
I must say
stop
and not busy my desires.

# NUYORICAN ANGEL OF WORDSMITHING

### (Note for a Poet)

I. Nuyorican Aesthetics:

It is a moral imperative to give poetry to the people. It is a media twenty-first-century picturetel event when a young poet can read on *Unplugged,* transferring via MTV the heat of passion. Electronic verse has changed the craft of writing poetry. We can interact *live* with Tokyo, London and Rome simultaneously; once the poet reaches millions, he/she learns how a verse can heal human pain.

II. Illness, Inspiration and Metaphor:

a. Use the first person instead of the third person if it isn't pathos.

b. Imaging Pain and Pleasure

i) without becoming maudlin or melodramatic;

ii) without eliciting pity from the reader; and

iii) provoke a feeling of interaction between the person who is ill or enraptured (the metaphor-maker) and the reader's imagination.

III. Cultural Worker: A Humble Servant

IV. Poet's Burial:

a. Instructions for ceremony should be written as a poem.

b. The community walks in a processional honoring its bard.

V. Meditation:

a. Concentration:          Empty the mind totally.

b. Analytical Concentration:    Put one objective in mind.

Keep all other concerns out.

# NUYORICAN ANGEL HYPERICIN

### (St. John's Wort)

I.

—"Close the shades, there's too much light in here,"
   says the Angel of Hypericin.

—"But it's the middle of the night,"
   Mitch responds.

—"Even cattle, sheep, goats and dogs know to screen the sun
   when I am present,"
   says the Angel of Hypericin.

II.

Mitch remembered the hope the Angel of Hypericin
brought to his parched future,
there was no cleansing rain expected,
no balm in sight,
but the Angel of Hypericin entered Mitch
in the form of scalding intra-venous infusions.
Hypericin came as a dark-brown fluid
in a thin metal needle with a sharp diagonal tip,
piercing the skin, entering the vein,
timed by a digital electronic plunger.

III.

The Angel first advances on the body as a hot,
tingling sensation that quickly becomes an
unbearable skin meltdown.
The Angel of Hypericin requires funereal darkness,
exposure to light burns the skin to the bone.
His visits were numerous, for almost a year.
In order to bear the Angel's balm,
his medicinal anger and anguish,
Mitch would avoid exposure to light, to cold,
to heat, to wind, even down to growing
increasingly terrified of turning on his kitchen light.


IV.

The Angel of Hypericin would punish the skin,
shake the body's temperature into violent
highs and lows,
within ten seconds Mitch would sweat or tremble with cold,
he remembered his first encounter,
it had taken the Angel twenty minutes to enter.
Mitch would look at the digital infusion plunger
then at his skin and then at the many clinical eyes
that could not hide their quest for results.
Not knowing what they were looking for
made their stare dispassionately distant,
and having to pretend that they were in control of the Angel
made their looks go from objective helplessness
to cagey stolen glances to see if the Angel
had exacted his price,

to see if Mitch in the middle of a bright,
sunlit day would ask,
"Isn't it odd the sun is out, not a cloud in the sky
and that it's raining so hard?"
Mitch felt soaked by a waterless downpour,
the Angel's presence made him feel
dizzyingly drenched by an invisible thunderstorm.
The Angel of Hypericin never visits alone,
he never comes without his digital plunger,
and one or two attendants to qualify and quantify
his painful balm.


V.

Mitch welcomed Hypericin's visits.
Three times per week the Angel would flow
through a stainless steel tunnel,
his entry always accompanied with electrical currents
moving like bamboo shoots beneath the fingernails.
Mitch's skin became more leathery with each visit.
Hypericin's possession of Mitch was accompanied by
electrical showers for which there were no conductors.
Mitch knew that Hypericin's visits
were a roast of the soul and of the self.

# NUYORICAN ANGEL PAPO

## (The Bi-Sexual Super Macho)

I.

The Fourth of July fireworks
went unseen by me.
If you could not see them
then I would not see
the New York skyline
ablaze in colored fire.
The red, white and blue
would climb to the moon
without my Fourth of July
Coney Island, Bushwick, Brooklyn
churchgoing,
newfound friend,
we parted in the name of fear,
the not falling into the black hole
of speedy passions
and underdeveloped love.
I drove you home,
shook your hand as we opened the trunk
to get your pack,
but you know, really,
I almost pushed you back
into the car, the hearth,
the fireplace of warmth,
the wheels that would have,
could have crossed the Williamsburg Bridge,
into Loisaida,
driven us into a nest of dreams
and corruption,

and purity and cleanliness
entwined in next to perfect lust,
yet, no, instead,
I didn't see the fireworks.
Instead, I sat thinking about
how nice it was to have left you
without our rushed desires fueling
the blazing Fourth of July skyline of New York.


II.

I tried
to separate
where we should start to touch.
I tried postponing, first with "Straight out of Brooklyn,"
then food,
but you were on an impulse
to burn fire,
to scorch passions,
I should've left you in Bushwick,
without numbers exchanged,
I could have lied about my name,
yet could'ves and would'ves
live in conditional tenements,
where on the third floor
we committed unconditional love,
knee to knee
nude from the waist down,
lust-fueled hands full
of belly buttons, buttocks and meat.

# NUYORICAN ANGEL OF EUTHANASIA

I. Serial Killer Angel

I was thirteen when I first
molested a young boy.
Then I began to kill.
I once stabbed one,
didn't realize it though.
I didn't know my knife had entered.
Later I found out it penetrated the stomach.
I fantasized about it everywhere,
even at work I just thought about
going to a school, a movie, a park,
it's what I wanted to do,
assault, rape, abuse young boys.
I am on death row,
if you want to let me out,
go ahead, but outside I'll just
keep doing it, within hours I'll
be after one, it's what I want to do.
If you set me free,
it's what I'm going to do,
so you might as well hang me,
or if you want, let me out,
but once out there I'll do what I want to do,
I'll kill another one.

II. Angel of Mercy

The rope prepared according
to State Department specifications
snapped his neck neatly.

The specs called for a specific knot
that would not let him linger,
it broke him like a twig.
His victims hadn't been so surgically killed,
his was a carefully planned suicide,
it wasn't justice, not really,
it was a man demanding to be killed
not out of remorse but a dare,
"Don't kill me and I'll do it again."
He staged his own suicide,
no ACLU eager esquire,
no madcap campaign against Capital Punishment
could stop him from throwing his glove down,
could stop his slap in the face,
his "I want to die and the State of Washington
will have to build a gallows and a trap door
'cause if it don't,
I'll do it again."
So you see, in the way of things,
in the round of peeling oranges,
he hung himself,
though he made the state
prepare the noose,
he committed legal suicide,
at the hands of the long arm
of a trap-door-pulling justice of the law.

# NUYORICAN ANGEL OF REVENGE

I. Nuyorican Poets Cafe

Stop, don't enter my temple,
I, Miky, from across the centuries
forbid you to enter,
no, no tanks will tear
the 3rd Street south wall
of my Nuyorican Poets Cafe.
No slam-bang-thank-you-mam
revolutionary will split
the arterial atom
of our cultural DNA,
no gene-splitting Bart Simpson skinheads
jangling silver skulls
and post–World War II dog tags will close my doors
No!
Stop!
You will not defile my temple,
you who are angered by racist juries
will not burn down my house
and, if I can help it,
you will not burn down your own,
move on out,
out there,
across the tracks,
your backyard is for burning leaves,
your homes are your safe-houses,
cross the boulevards
burn the other, whatever the other is,
it might be the green of a manicured lawn,
the blue Azaleas grown for cutting,
break other windows, not mine,

for I, like you,
have been abused by time and chance,
rage, rage, rage
but not against yourselves.
No!
No, the first local loco that breaks
the rules of my temple
will be stopped on site,
and back-hand-slapped
till the bandit crosses the tracks
without entering my temple,
so what's the body count now?
Small businesses wracked and ruined
so that four low-life homeboys
can sleep at home tonight—
is it worth it America?
White driver stoned with chunks of glass and concrete
with the return of the not-guilty verdict?


II. Angel of Brutality

Carnage, victims, the living dead
a foregone conclusion?
The red-hot-poker urge for peace,
for the illusion of justice,
denied by camcorder record of brutality?
But no stonewalling the bruise-covered Rodney King,
face busted, leg broken,
and "not that much damage done."
Thirty times the jury watched the tape,
fifty-six blows connected,

it was junk justice,
and righteous anger
with wrongful marauders defiling,
knowing that victims
find that truth gets them nowhere.
The killer of Federico Perreira
cleared by a jury,
is hailed as a conquering hero—
burn down the village,
but not ours, not yours,
not this time,
burn Gary Spath's home,
the dumb-as-dirt jerk
that shot Teaneck's 14-year-old in the back,
burn in Brooklyn
where Hector Rivera, Jr.
cannot get a grand jury
to hand down an indictment
for his father's death,
who was killed by a rookie cop,
let all marauders rot in cells
along with those stonewalling
police-conduct investigations,
let's not salute rogue cops
while we've still got a country left.
Stop, don't enter my temple!

# DEUTSCHE NUYORICAN ANGELS

I. Tacheles

Façade squatted
by young Berliners
in the Jewish quarters,
Mitch's head buzzes
with war sirens warning
of a blitz, a showering of metal explosives,
eagle-eyed bombs
making bright blazing paths
towards the tribe of Israel's ghettos.
It's 1997, the end of the century
and the empty ruins are now
theme bars,
discos,
makeshift lived-in businesses,
the rear of the building is
pure space, transparent,
not a girder in sight,
no tools, work benches,
merchandise, nothing,
the rear of the building is a dusty parcel of land,
just a memory now,
down the street the restored synagogue
where Kristallnacht began,
the shell of the temple
resplendent in its gold gilded stone
belies an utterly empty interior,
the gutted out house of Jewish worship
wears a painted face
without a pew in which to pray,
the face of Berlin is

a packed house of hip,
some beat, some alive
sharpshooters
that will take your breath away,
if you aren't ready
for how rich they are,
how on the pulse
of NOW—
a German dj
reads some rap in English
and he tips,
"it's too not happening here,
I'm tipping."
That could have been
a run-in with a Lower East Side
denizen too bored with life
to signify,
apply the self,
and work the space.


II. Schwarze Angels

African-German diaspora,
can there be Turkish pride?
What's happened
to ethnic purity?
It's there,
the Simpsons don't see it,
don't even dream it—
but moving on,
Mitch learned to pass synagogues

guarded by automatic rifles
yes,
it was Germany
which won the war
not the Allied forces of Europe.

# NUYORICAN ANGEL OF DESPAIR

**(December 31, at the End of the Millennium)**

So free that liberty weighs 'round my neck,
so without restraint that ropes tie my mind to Somalia,
so world-wide-bright-eyed gone wild
that Africa is the brilliant white-and-black
of an opaque 1934 Tarzan flick,
a dream that rides me to the burial grounds
so I couldn't leave my house till Ted Koppel
showed me how valiantly the U.S. Somalian
relief operation yields the best
Channel 7 Eyewitness Nightline News
foreign occupation television special.
I couldn't leave my house, so I didn't get to find out
if my date was a he or a she
cross-dressed either way.
You see, I've already seen *The Crying Game*
and I'm not taking bets on who's a she or he,
but forget that,
do you know what surprised the Marines,
it wasn't Somalians,
it was a sea of extra-terrestrial lights
and television pre-occupation news teams,
"It's an eerie sight," said a two-star general
as he arranged his would-be-presidential hair
for a 2000 run for the White House T.V. shot.
It isn't that the Somalians need food and relief,
you see, we also need great T.V. viewing
and Allah knows that we have to have it,
and Allah delivers,
the warlords perform in the theater of operations,
yes, Allah is great,
so during the morning talk shows we're dismayed

by how our kids are traumatized
by skeletal two-, three-, ten-year-old Somalian children—
what counseling should we do for them?
Well maybe the good samaritan thing to do
is turn the T.V. off and let your child eat,
then turn it on again
when you want to see the great moral
imperative of our armed nation
dump Marines on a lit beach
with a civilian army of world correspondents
eagerly waiting with microphones in hands
while our Marines crawl on their bellies
up to the microphones to say,
"Hey, these Africans don't have bullets,
they're just hungry."

# SHARED LOVE

## (Bio/Ethics in an Age of Plagues)

# P R O E M

## ii

*I*nfirmities take over the body without warning or proclamation. The potential for infection is endless and the capacity for the body to restrain and combat the armies of trillions of cells that would destroy the biological balance and health of the body is, at best, limited. Very often, the body's defenses are helpless.

We have known the power of plagues from the beginning of time. It is not new to die by the hundreds of thousands. It is often hunger that claims whole populations. However, in the late twentieth century it is not hunger alone that is responsible for mass death, but viruses. These viruses have a capacity for mutating so rapidly that medication is rendered useless before it can successfully treat the symptoms or help the body retrieve its innate fighting capacity. In the face of this biological warfare, we must devise a moral field that defines our behavior towards each other. There are plagues carried by the air—in those cases, we quarantine the bearer. There are, on the other hand, plagues that can be controlled if we use personal restraint and care in how we meet to share love with each other.

# HIV

## I.
### Revelation

*To tell in strength. "The telling," when to tell, leads to a discovery between the teller and the listener. Acquiring knowledge; the teller holds his/her information as a tool for health, movement towards truth.*

## II.
### Salvation

*To converse as an attempt to recuperate, a holding on not to die.*

## III.
### Speech

*To acquire "language" for talking about a plague in the self.*

## IV.
### Sharing Secrets

*Who to tell? Is there someone? The search for what to tell.*

## V.
### Mature Masculinity

*Welcome the responsibility to do the work of building verbs, adjectives and nouns for mortality and its subsequent eternal breaking of concrete.*


### I. Revelation

Revel at ion,
rebel at I on a course
to regret erections,
to whip the cream in my scrotum
till it hardens into unsweetened,
unsafe revved elations

of milk turned sour
by the human body,
of propagation of destruction.
The epiphany: I am unsafe,
you who want me
know that I who want you,
harbor the bitter balm of defeat.

II. *Salvation*

If I were to show you
how to continue holding on,
I would not kiss you,
I would not mix my fluids with yours,
for your salvation
cannot bear the live weight
of your sharing liquids with me.

III. *Language*

To tell,
to talk,
to tongue into sounds
how I would cleanse you with urine,
how my tasting tongue would wash your body,
how my saliva and sperm would bloat you,
to touch you in our lovemaking
and not tell you
would amount to murder.
To talk about how to language this

so that you would still languish
in my unsafe arms and die,
seems beyond me,
I would almost rather lie
but my tongue muscle moves involuntarily
to tell of the danger in me.


IV. *Of Health*

To use my full and willing
body to reveal and speak
the strength that I impart
without fear,
without killing,
without taking away what I would give,
to use my man's tongue
to share,
to give,
to lend,
to exact nothing,
to receive all things,
to expand my macho
and let the whole world
into the safety of my mature masculinity.


V. *Quarantine*

Sometimes I fear touching your plump ear lobes,
I might contaminate you.
Sometimes I refuse odors that would

drive my hands to spread your thick thighs.
Sometimes closing my ears to your voice
wrenches my stomach and I vomit to calm wanting.
Can it be that I am the bearer of plagues?
Am I poison to desire?
Do I have to deny yearning for firm full flesh
so that I'll not kill what I love?
No juices can flow 'tween you and me.
Quicksand will suck me in.

# VIH

## I.
### Revelación

*Decir mientras hay fuerza. "El decir," cuando decirlo conduce hacia un descubrimiento entre el narrador y el que escucha. Adquirir conocimiento; el narrador retiene su información como a una herramienta de salud, un movimiento hacia la verdad.*

## II.
### Salvación

*Conversar cual movimiento hacia la recuperación, algo de que agarrarse para no morir.*

## III.
### El Habla

*Tomar la palabra para hablar sobre la plaga en uno mismo.*

## IV.
### Compartiendo Secretos

*¿A quién contarle? ¿Habrá alguien? La busqueda de el qué decir.*

## V.
### Madurez Masculina

*Bienvenida la responsabilidad de trabajar construyendo verbos, adjetivos y nombres para la muerte y su subsecuente eterna ruptura de lo concreto.*

I. *Revelación*

Juerga en ion,
rebelarme contra mí mismo en el transcurso
de lamentar erecciones,
de batir la crema de mis testículos

hasta que se endurezca desabrida,
regocijo acelerado y peligroso
de leche cortada
por el cuerpo humano,
de propagación, de destrucción.
La epifanía: ¡Soy peligroso!
tú que me quieres
avisate que yo,
el que te quiere,
albergo el amargo bálsamo de la derrota.


## II. *Salvación*

Si te mostrara
como continuar resistiendo,
no te besaría,
ni mezclaría los fluidos
de mi cuerpo contigo;
pues tu salvación
no puede cargar el peso vivo
de nuestro intercambio de líquidos.


## III. *Lenguaje*

Para decir,
para hablar,
para darle lengua a los sonidos,
cómo limpiarte con orines,
cómo bañarte el cuerpo con mi lengua golosa,
cómo hincharte con mi saliva y mi esperma,

tocarte en el acto de amor
y no decirtelo
sería un asesinato,
hablar de cómo articular esto
para que todavía pudieras languidecer
en mis brazos peligrosos y morir,
está fuera de mí,
casi preferiría mentir,
pero el músculo de mi lengua se mueve involuntariamente
para hablar del peligro que hay en mí.


IV. *Sobre la Salud*

Usar mi cuerpo lleno y capaz
para revelar y hablar
de la fuerza que yo imparto
sin miedo,
sin matar,
sin desviar lo que daría
por usar mi lengua de hombre
para compartir,
dar,
prestar,
demandar nada,
para recibirlo todo
para expandir mi hombría
y dejar al mundo entero
entrar en la seguridad de mi madurez masculina.

## V. *Cuarentena*

A veces me da miedo
tocar el lóbulo gordezuelo de tu oreja,
porque podría contaminarte.
A veces rechazo olores
que conduzcan mis manos a separar tus muslos gruesos.
A veces cerrar mis oidos a tu voz
me revuelve el estómago y vomíto
para calmar las ganas.
¿Será verdad que soy el portador de plagas?
¿Seré yo veneno para el deseo?
¿Tendré que negarme
el apetito por la carne firme y completa
para no matar lo que amo?
Ningun líquido puede fluir entre nosotros,
solamente las arena movediza
me tragarán.

Traducción de Sandra A. García

# SHEETS

I thought I had seen the last,
the end of love's orgasm,
but she held on to the tar thread
that my moist love impulse had become
on that rainy March Monday,
when for the first-neon-light moment
I was told of killer dark-red-cells
circumnavigating my life line.
She held tight,
no nonsense here she said,
love saves the day,
so let us make do,
   let us invent
magic touches in tubercular time.
She held her body proud,
not bound by coquettish charm,
she held her love upright,
till I one morning woke
into her "I won't let you hide" hugs
and turns and legs upright
perpendicular to the bed
yes, she brought me back
to the sheet of breath
that connects sperm and egg,
that blends guilt and love
into rushing for towels
to wipe the demon of desire
from her thighs, from her breasts,
from her,
demons away from her,
thighs not milked by me,
life not threatened,

wipe, wipe, wipe,
wipe the sperm,
get it off the sheets,
off her,
off our love,
off, off, off,
off with the plague.
What? An orgasm?
How dare I?

# PENNSYLVANIA LOVE

A childlike pleasure,
the nascent flush of an erection,
in that child's walk too,
are the innocent clutches.
A walk in a Pennsylvania woods,
the not knowing, the undressing,
to wash in a clear brook's water,
the twenty-five-mile hike
to a green forest's solitude,
where palpable lust yields
to sweeter inhibitions
and quieter liquid limp brushes
of genitalia, elbows, arms,
thighs and lips,
there our five senses blend into a beehive
of honeyed gropings for love.

# FOR J.R.

When I realized I loved you,
it was too late to take your hand out,
wrench it from the grip it had on my heart,
I would have spurned your bed,
spat on your face.
Instead I fell
like a stupid yo-yo
right to the end of my rope,
without rebound to climb
up that cotton thread
back to myself,
where I could've fought you off,
never letting on that I couldn't move
without holding on
to your firm alabaster body,
never letting you know
that it was not glamorous
to dream of white limbs
spread-eagled over my brown body,
wrong, it was wrong,
white on brown should be left
to Skippy Peanut Butter
on White Wonder Bread.

# LOVE FOOD

Solid carat carrot love,
good and pungent toe radish,
cool cucumber salad sheet sandwich,
smoke boneless flesh on rye,
love over fried zucchini,
genitals awash in hollandaise sauce,
calamari fritti dripped in head cheese,
eggplant-grilled flaming hearts,
tongue sandwiched 'tween burning vaginal lips,
love fungus grown in dark sweaty groins,
freshly squeezed sweat juice
quenches my thirst.

# INWARD SLIDE

Trying to color wash the afternoon,
striking at hidden shadows,
snow-knives piercing concrete,
he didn't always get the hang
of nana moments,
he growled at sweet melodies,
the song of the river forgot him,
the sinking tide wouldn't wash
his deep confusion to the other shore,
all smelled bitter and tasted of salt,
the sunrise bore lazy rays
and wrapped his muddied sight
to his inner thighs,
it was an inward dive
that brought on torrential
waves of bio-chemical depression.

# AUGUST IN LOISAIDA

**(August in the Lower East Side)**

iii

*F*rom Delancey to 14th Street, from Third Avenue to the FDR Drive, lies the neighborhood known as Loisaida. Tens of languages are spoken on literally every block. And, though covered by tar and concrete, the yards of our tenement houses are filled with bushes, flowers and fruit trees.

Loisaida has changed much. In the 1950s, when I was a child, my mother had me fetch our daily quart of milk from the dairy storefront run by Mr. Schervina. He in turn got his milk from the back of the store, where he kept his ten milk-cows. Walking down Avenue C, I could inhale the smells of the Italian foodstands, and then pick some fruit from the open-air fruit stall. On Orchard Street, I watched the clothes-vendors carry their wares on horse-drawn carriages, and then later the horses walk unhitched in teams of twenty back to their stables. On Sundays I liked to observe the Jews and Puerto Ricans, who traveled to the blintz-shops on First Avenue, where they ordered matzoh-ball soup and drank tea served in glasses with a wedge of lemon.

•   •   •

While things have changed since then, we residents of Loisaida still cook homemade jams and share them with our neighbors and lovers. Once lost love is often rediscovered here in our barrio. Loisaida is our home, a place to mourn the loss of the major players on the streets of Loisaida, too often fallen to the plagues of violence and illness.

# AUGUST 9

(Se Murio el Poeta)

When he jumped to the beat of the drum
the mirror spat back at him
in envy of his pure feelings,
he felt his pulse searching
for infusions of attention,
his motion dance
spun more webs
than spiders on a sunny August afternoon
where endless light
illuminates all objective details
clearing the impulses of the breath
for each step the dancer takes.

# AUGUST 10

## (Michael's Visit)

Michael calls through the window
to find me alone,
in between telephone calls and people,
I read a poem asking if it's poetry.
Michael responds, giving me the sign,
showing he remembers
what my words transmitted.

# AUGUST 11

## (Mitch & Michael: A Dodge '77 Trot)

I turn her over gently,
three depressions jetting gas into her carburetor,
buckled in and feeling safe.
I ride Michael to the West Side sunbathing pier
listening for sounds of malfunctions.

Like the time I smelled the gas
when I first filled her up,
leaving the U.S. Route 1 Dodge dealership
to drive downtown New Brunswick
with a full tank I'd gotten at the Sunoco
only to set a tall, frontally bald man on fire.

The tank was leaking a steady flow of gas
that collected while I ran in
and out of my insurance broker's office
so that when the tall bald man
who was lighting his cigarette
pitched the match,
a poof of gas flared up singeing his eyebrows.
I apologized, drove off to the dealer,
who promised quick service,
no cost, that's too bad, come back at five.
I did, found tank parts replaced,
was told engine was tuned,
that wasn't true,
but that seems to be the real in business deals,
got towed outside the Holland Tunnel,
the gas gauge was stuck on half tank
though the tank was empty.
Now the brake light's not working,

the idle is off, the glove compartment door
springs open over any serious city bump
and this morning the engine exhaust
was milk-white in color,
but here I'm at it again
buckled into my seat,
showing the machine off to Michael
as we ride west on Third St.
over to the pier and down south
to Ken and John's in SoHo
to drink an hour away.

# AUGUST 12

Was visited by Willie and Ernie,
talked, drank coffee, saw Joey,
got a call from August to move the car
by 11 o'clock or else pay the city twenty-five,
left my key with the super
so he could let the man in to plaster
the bathroom wall which is crumbling
all around the shower,
decided to let Willie take Ernie home,
practice driving for his test next week,
stopped at Ernie's for two hours,
came back to 524 E. 6th St.,
found August smashing glass all over the house,
I asked why,
he said he was looking at Yvonne's photo portrait
of us and that he "punched it,"
every glass in the dish sink was shattered,
I turned around to walk out,
he smashed the electric typewriter with a swift kick,
I hesitated saying,
"please go and leave the keys."
As I started the truck I could still hear breaking glass,
came back two hours later,
found the fan toppled over on the floor,
the motor torn from its holder,
the door was left ajar,
the keys weren't left behind,
no word from him since yesterday . . .

# AUGUST 13

Awoke remembering I was alone
in the anger-glow of severed love,
felt green remorse in the amber light
of the rising sun, watched feelings in me
like I watch the peaches in the yard,
from day to day their ripening yellow
comes to full glow in August sun,
haven't seen him since the night of the 12th,
when the last words I heard were in the breaking glass.

# AUGUST 14

It isn't a woman.
It isn't a man.
August is lush green heat
with scattered rays of light
that scamper through dark gray clouds.
The mass of my flesh is constipated,
fluids move molasses heavy.
Throughout the color of the moment,
the touch of things threatens
to expose how full of fear
in the lush green month of August I can be.
Slept forty-five minutes,
fear sets in when nobody's present.
I'm never alone,
a muted trumpet
releases melodies to all my unrehearsed disasters
as August brings the sweetest juices from the land,
dispersing fruits and harvest bushels
to the poet and the farmer who have worked.

# AUGUST 15

August visited the working poet
in New York fields where tar is plowed.
I prescribed a balm of harvest amber
that mixed with sky blue and August light,
creates the golden wheat stalks
poets store to survive the winter solstice.

# AUGUST 16

### (Irma's Indio)

Este indio
pide misericordia divina,
su poder corre en su meditación
sobre la carga diaria
que cansa sus músculos
y lleva el sol
adentro de su cansancio.

# AUGUST 16

## (Irma's Indio)

This Indian
prays for divine mercy,
his power runs through meditations
on the daily hardships
that strain his muscles,
as he calls on the sun
to soothe his exhaustion.

Translation by Sandra A. García

# AUGUST 17

## (Maria y Miguel)

Maria and Miguel went to San Juan
for four days to push Maria's poetry and music,
Tia Delia told Maria that her poetry talks
and that she admired her for the poem to Juncos,
though she felt that it could have been longer.
Maria nearly wept when Tia Delia's eyes got moist,
over Maria's poem to her son Arturo:

*"se que muy lejos estás de mí, hijo adorado,*
*pero aun asi, mas cerca de mí te siento,*
*nunca ceso de pensar en tí, y te llevo en mi pensamiento,*
*siento que la distancia aun nos sigue separando."*

Everywhere Maria went people talked about her book of poems.
She smiled butterflies remembering
Tia Delia minding her speech,
choosing her words more carefully this visit
though she felt "people shouldn't really do that"
since she'd only gone to the sixth grade in Puerto Rico,
but she did smile deep when she thought of it,
and humble too, she enjoyed the idea of it,
the care of it, wanting to sound it right to feeling,
that's what made Maria smile,
that she had earned the respect to be talked to right,
it all made sense to people that Maria had a voice,
that her talent would out
but that it would all come down at fifty-seven,
that's shower of gold,
and when her music came,
all those songs she sang into a tape recorder
paid off, since everywhere

she played her tape
people danced and felt her beat.
After the music came to her she traveled.
She went to see Arturo in Hawaii last year,
but Miguel's afraid she's running
forty-eight hours into twenty-four,
so he slows her down, his way has time not speed,
and hers has energy not patience, she realized her drive
is to put it down, to let herself all the way through
to page and music sheet.
Miguel is proud his woman is strong,
they're going to Pauilo, to Arturo's house again,
I'm sending him a fetish Native Americans use
to neutralize short-circuits in the spine,
Miguel and Maria are off again,
many miles from the island
where they were born.

Peach picking time
at 524 E 6th St.,
asked Lois if she'd want to make peach pies
for everybody after I pick them tomorrow,
sitting on a Sunday afternoon,
eating peaches, watching Sandy's daughter Cristina discover
the backyard, Miranda and Hero sunning themselves
on the window ledge, Augie was to call to spend the day,
the August heat relents for an afternoon of pleasure,
talking to Sandy and Lois about Sandy's
short piece for Belle Star to play Chuleria
an intellectual Russian-Jewish street woman
who rocks rock 'n' roll into your heart,
Lois didn't answer yet,
I wonder if she'll cook the peaches.
In her one-scene piece,
Sandy's still on her idea of the clown
as the protagonist of life.
Cristina smears tofu carob almond sponge cake all over her face
as the Beatles pour out of Bo's third-floor rear window.
August light lighter than light
finds me in flight towards Miguel and Maria
before they jet off to Hawaii.
I drive wondering how many peaches are on the tree,
I'll know tomorrow,
maybe Lois will preserve them,
they're ripe but only certain angles in the yard
provide them enough light
they're almost sweet though,

August light plus green makes sweet juice flow,
peach picking time
at 524 E 6th St.
If Lois doesn't cook them for our winter eat,
I guess I could stew and jar them.

# AUGUST 19

### (Penalty)

If you did it
then say you did it
and you pay for it,
but if you didn't do it
and it can be proven that you did do it
then you say you did it and you cop a plea,
however, if you did do it
but doubt can be proven that you didn't do it
then say you didn't and you just don't pay for it.

# AUGUST 20

August visited, came in and watered the plants,
picked up his umbrella, jacket
and plastic bag with tomatoes.
"Stay a while," I asked him.
He shrugged meekly saying,
"I don't live here anymore
and why are there three cans of catfood open?"
I answered that I kept pushing goods into the fridge
and that the cans kept disappearing.
Augie then asked about the bathroom.
I said Willie covered the bathroom wall
with N. Y. Times job advertisements during the afternoon
and waterproofed the paper by tacking the clear plastic tarp
I bought for three dollars with the nails
Frank left behind before he split for Wisconsin.
Augie looked about and waved me goodbye.
I gave the phone over to Richie Cruz
so that he could rap to Miky
who was calling from L.A.
and walked over to Augie
who glowed sun-tan brown
while his eyes lighter than light
read that I was missing
the merry month and point
of August again.
"Hug the cats, they need a lot of hugging," he said.

4:30 A.M. Lina calls,
"I've been raped, I called the police
now I'm calling you."
Coming to, I hear her cry and talk
till the police arrive and take her to the hospital.
I didn't get an address from Lina so I sat and thought
and felt the ordeal, from house to precinct,
to hospital for penicillin
and the semen sample the rape squad
requires for charges to stick.
Called her at 9:30 in the morning,
she'd been back from the hospital since 8:30 A.M.,
penetration against desire,
sensual betrayal spewing unwanted seeds,
prying, wedging, invading her body.
Called Lina back at 2:30 P.M., Nellie was there
I was glad that she got there
but felt vulnerable for not getting to her first,
hung up and went to Brooklyn to fill Lina's prescription.
She was already walking down the street with Nellie
to get the anti-pregnancy pills herself,
she's walking slower today
as if to shed the hurt in her.

# AUGUST 22

Want to see myself
through to the end
of every day,
before sleep conquers
my need to touch flesh.

# AUGUST 23

I feel calm, at ease,
as opposed to aficiado, choked,
driven, distressed, phone rings,
Richard's voice sounds fresh, relieved,
on a calm almost fall day in late August.
I stretch my feelings into *The Realm of the Senses*
to find that obsession with pleasure ends in death,
to lose my bet with Willie that we wouldn't
be aroused by the film,
to come home at 6:30 P.M. to talk with August,
who beams rays of independent beauty
as I slide in and out of the consuming want to make love
and the rejuvenating need
to create variations on that theme,
there is a word for the smell of love
and it isn't funky, rancid or foul,
sex smells of pain and its color is blood red.

# AUGUST 24

## (Michael's Reading)

Wish there were a mystery that would out
but as this day unravels
I keep finding familiarity more constant
than mysteries and new feelings.
Rose on time, dressed late, ate early,
the day's here, on call, get it on,
don't mess around,
don't be afraid of secretless sun ups or downs,
by the day's end constant familiarity
will bring you to Michael's reading
for unfamiliar words about
Jeronimo riding his ten-speed bike
delivering lox and bagels
to professional Puerto Ricans
who have newly moved to the Grand Concourse,
Michael claims he forgot his name,
maybe I'll send him a note with Michael written on it,
maybe he'll misunderstand my intention
and throw an eggplant at me,
wish there were a mystery that would out
of Michael's right eye and disappear into his left.

# AUGUST 25

**(Joey's Pride)**

"I'm never going to be short of food
'cause every Friday I buy forty dollars worth,
without food coupons either,
I mean I buy a solid forty
with my sweat and dollars."

# AUGUST 26

## (Backyard)

Qualita Superiore 1975, Soave
we almost didn't buy it, too expensive,
but Michael hesitated so we bought it.
Two glasses into the Soave Michael finds
that there's a peach hue
to the backyard air
that fills the space between Lobito, Michael and myself,
wanted to ask Lobito if he felt the light between us
but I held back afraid that he'd say no,
Lois is inside cooking the peaches I picked
day before yesterday, readying the peach jam,
tomorrow we'll sterilize the jars, melt the wax
to seal bacteria out and decide
who gets Sixth Street homegrown peach jam,
preserved for warm winter toast.

# AUGUST 27

## (Phebe's)

Drinks with Lobito,
plans to use his Master Charge,
but can't find it,
it's not on him,
can we walk out without explosions?
The heat is on,
the plastic's melting,
the manager walks up to us,
Lobito says he might've left the card
with the bartender two nights ago,
"oh, well you can't find it,
you'll have to leave your driver's license."
Lobito raps that he doesn't drive,
but that he's got a Citicard,
"well, I'll keep your Citicard until tomorrow."
We both slip back into our drinks and talk,
I wonder if Lobito will go back for his Citicard
or trade it in for $7.89.

# AUGUST 28

Warm Sunday, boiled the peaches a full eight hours,
nearly burned them waiting for the jam to thicken,
turned out moist, spreads smoothly
and gently spiced by Lois,
Sandy stops by on her way to
The Family's Brooklyn Festival,
"The Children Shall Lead Them."
Went to Brooklyn, dropped Sandy, Willie, Lobito, Cristina,
drove back to Manhattan to Sixth St.,
stopped at my place for a service call
Irma needed to make, drove back to Brooklyn
in the presence of the full moon.
At the irreverent cross of Jay and Gold streets,
Chekov's Russian comic romp through marriage rituals
explodes in a hilarious Caribbean world
where Ivan Garcia keeps his land and woman too.
Sat next to Pancho God and felt it too,
I mean I saw how he is the source of rhythm,
cutting in there, right at the comic heart
of Ivan's love for Natalia,
and Chekov's plot, the way Pancho God
made the dog controversy mean to the crowd
by calling forth the ghost of Cantinflas,
everybody knows Cantinflas had a short lower jaw.
My red Hawaiian shirt with the white seahorses
had retained the sweet smell of boiling peaches
so that when Natalia came on stage looking like Hercules
the seahorses in my shirt swam for joy.
Pancho reads Chekov's "Marriage Proposal"
back to its universal bone,
back to where it's a man and it's a woman
and they're into accounting

for what each brings to the other
before I becomes We
and Papa can die in peace,
spin, spin faster and faster
into outer Caribbean space with saxophones, drums,
spin faster yet when you can
outstrip, melt down, dismiss the bag
of "urban ex-convicts theatre therapy group"
and crack open New York hearts with an old,
classic Russian comedy
at the heart of which there's a director/man
who times pain into theatrical pleasure.

# AUGUST 29

(In Juan's Words)

"My father had T.B. and for two years
he waved at me till
the bus rode me out of sight
and what I find out now
is that they were experimenting
instead of treating him.
My mother made the trip
for two years before he died,
her man gave his life to the Experiments,
they're still doing it,
'sign this' but they don't give you
all the details of how his liver
got shot with drugs that made him
deteriorate into mush, intravenously fed.
That's the corner where I used to take the bus
to the Welfare Island Hospital
for last-minute looks
before his death got certified
at Seaview Hospital in Staten Island."

# AUGUST 30

## (Speed: The Bus Chase)

Rode to City Island early this morning,
drove down the three-lane highway
that leads up to the bay where greasy seafood's
served with August moonlight as the tide moves in.
Internally my muscles churn like boiling water
while outside, the bay lies waiting
for the action of a motor boat.
Inside the tiger climbs up my spine, clawing nerves,
leaving them to bleed internal sorrows and pain
as the full moon plays jacks with my memories,
reminding me of the bus chase
on the night of the 28th,
down the streets of Manhattan, bus driver
reaching for his gun, Willie cut the bus off
when making a left onto Varick,
the driver threw the bus into reverse
and gave chase, Willie made a sharp right
round the rear of the bus, I looked back to see a speeding
New York City Metropolitan Transit Authority bus
gaining ground on our rear,
Lobito laughing and toking,
Willie uncertain, not sure,
we turned right onto Washington St.,
Willie still unsure, "give it gas, he's gaining ground!"
turns left on Perry, Willie couldn't turn freely,
it was narrow, he's just learning to drive,
my new '77 copper Dodge van is wide,
Willie slowed to a halt,
the bus driver threw on his emergency brake,
ran out of the bus, but we made our turn,
and gassed our way down Perry St.,

I kept looking back,
saw how he ran back to the bus
and watched us reach the end of the block
where we turned under the West Side Highway,
he held vigil till we curved left
and sped south round the tip of the island,
past the Staten Island Ferry back to Sixth St.

# AUGUST 31

(St. Mark's on the Bowery)

I.

Sitting at 10th and Second Ave.,
across the cobblestoned plaza
lies the East Yard of St. Mark's on the Bowery.
Two or three pounds of corn grains
fill in the cracks between the stones,
winos, junkies and smartly dressed women and men,
inhabit the littered plaza, lined by four benches
on the southwest sidewalk,
the sky, gray, threatening rain.
"Let it pour and pour and pour," said the woman behind me.

II.

Walking west on 12th St.,
I called Michael to his window.
He yawned and waved though sleep
had drained the projective verse from his brow.

III.

There's a woman on the 4th floor of 166 2nd Ave.,
right over M. Horowitz's sign-painters' supply store,
who's been sitting there since I was twelve,
I suspect she had a toilet
built by the window.

Once I sat and watched her for thirteen hours,
she never moved,
I finally broke the spell
because I had to go pee.
Not she.


IV.

Sitting in the St. Mark's Church Square,
lost in thought when a seven-year-old boy cried
because his mother was stoned and didn't want to go home,
stopped waiting and left when his mother
wouldn't take him to the bathroom.
She whistled me over,
asked if I'd take him across the street
to the johns at the Greek's greasy spoon,
because she was waiting for her boyfriend.
We crossed the street, he was shy, pulling back,
got to the john, I stayed outside
till he called, asked if I'd help,
I said yes, he showed me his pants
smeared and stinking, he had had
to go he said, it wasn't his fault,
he couldn't hold anymore, I washed
his pants as he talked and washed himself,
crossed him over to the northwest side of 10th St.,
asked him if wet pants felt uncomfortable,
"yes but less smelly," he said.

# IV

# NUYORICAN
# KADDISH

# P R O E M

## iv

We come into the world naked, nurtured and protected because the world around us can devour us physically and mentally. We are helpless, in need of support, caresses, and kisses. It takes a long time for a human being to be self-sufficient and capable of self-defense.

We also begin our life at the same time that we begin to die. Biological attacks and deterioration happen from the inside out. As we come into our greatest mental and physical form, we also start the downgrade into old age and deterioration. Facing this, we embrace life in order to meet death in our private historical landscape, our sense of the immortal "I AM."

# forGet

forget Tito Puente riffing on his timbales,
forget Ray Barretto,
forget Rubén Blades,
forget Chano Pozo,
forget Perez Prado,
forget the best of Xavier Cugat,
forget Celia Cruz and her basso profundo voice,
forget Agustin Lara,
forget Sylvia Rexach,
forget Bobby Capo,
forget Ismael Rivera,
forget Cortijo,
forget it, just for get it.

# RED BLOOD FATHER

Dopa pills are white,
my father's fingers tan,
I'm sickly yellow in my longing
for his bright blue brash come back
through fluffy gray, white clouds.

It's mid-night black
to see him all interred in a box
of dull brown wood.
Let clear, loud sounds
announce his green return to health.
Let red run over wet brown soil,
when his blood returns to crimson life and joy.

# FLAT DROPS

Sunlight blue stains,
whether the rain brings magic
or builds up mudslides
that choke the memory into flatlines.

# DREAM WITH FATHER

I'm traveling on a train,
my dad walks up to me
and hands me a manuscript.
I am surprised, "How did
you get time for this?"
He talks about having time.
I tuck the manuscript into my bag,
the train pulls into the station,
I get confused about my coat.
By the time I spot it,
my father has vanished.

# TALKING TO THE OTHER SIDE
## OF THE FLATLINE

You didn't kiss me when you went,
no me besastes,
me dejastes solo sin un beso,
but the God of the Second Chance
blesses me and I know that
you will kiss me again,
that you will appear to me,
transform and re-new me.
You didn't kiss me when you went,
but you will kiss me when you come,
talking to the other side of the flatline,
crossing the line of death,
speaking to the God of the Second Chance,
joyful as you pierce my darkness.
Yes, you didn't kiss me when you left
but you'll kiss me in the second coming
as you resurrect in me and we find love
in the God of the Second Chance.

# FATHER AT ZERO-POINT-PLACE

I.

My mother's pleading voice, not resigned,
sang a crying song wishing for a rebirth,
my uncle, weeping for the first time
in my memory, sobbed,
"His eyes are open he's still looking at me,
you better get over here, I don't know what
to do, we've lost him."
I transformed each telephone word
into concrete objects:
I was there looking at father's soft skin,
touching his gentle lips,
caressing his still warm hands and fingers,
craving for a breath to escape him,
tricking myself into feeling his air
pressing on my cheek,
running my hands over his body,
looking for the warm spots,
his belly's hot,
his armpits still lukewarm,
his thighs, grown so thin, beginning to be cold,
my hands grab at his feet,
not yet icy cold,
I run my hands into his groin,
and there I find body heat, I find
his scrotum still simmers with an
amber temperature, his penis still
holds a glow, his buttocks
are now room temperature,
there is still a chance for a revival.

His eyes involuntarily open,
will he stand up and walk
among the sinners and the ill?
Will he continue to walk the earth beatified,
spreading saintliness
just as he had during my youth?
A kinder man lived only in books,
father's feather-weight touch
opened all of us to a fault,
because nowhere else were we ever loved
so gently and so fairly,
he was a judge with mercy and kindliness
in his heart
and understanding and balance were his law,
he knew that at the heart of law was generosity
and that mercy made human contracts work,
here was a Daniel, a Solomon,
a worthy homespun philosopher of family justice.
Yes, there is still a chance for a revival,
the rebirth that takes place in the mind.


II.

I've already found my Deep-Space Nine photograph,
but mother spins an endless reel,
she cannot stop to cradle a single frame,
she keeps on running the tape
of her fifty-seven years with him,
re-playing their never having slept a single night apart,
the reel to real joy of eternally

rejuvenating happiness in married partnership,
the video of never having been lonely,
or alone or without her man,
without his warming her slippers
so that they wouldn't be cold to her feet,
or cooking his special diet to cure her ulcer,
his buttoning her blouse
or pulling up her zipper,
his patience with her mental break-ups,
or the way in which he crossed his legs
when company arrived,
but the reel that drives mother hauntingly wild
is the empty bed, life without him,
even the seventy-five-pound
more fragile than frail body
that his wasted frame had become was her man,
still there, needing his pillows,
her hand to brush his teeth,
his feces cleaned and removed,
needing his enemas, needing his spit suctioned,
needing his liquid food,
cleaning his intestinal tube
through which traveled medication and nourishment,
yes, that's the real reel,
the non-occupied space,
the zero-point-place,
the nobody in space and place,
that's the terror Uncle Al
experienced this morning,
that's the tremor that rocked mother,
they both awoke hoping a dream had passed,
that the zero-point nobody-in-place-space

had evaporated, that father's
more fragile than frail body
would still be there.


III.

Mother and Uncle Al
arose hoping that the police
had not been there,
the death certificate
had not been signed,
hoping the body
had not been picked up
by the La Paz Funeral Parlor embalmer,
who made a southbound turn
onto the northbound traffic on Queens Boulevard
with my father's cadaver
neatly tucked into a body bag
in the rear of his station wagon
which I was following,
furiously blowing my horn,
waving my hands,
screaming, whistling,
frantically blinking my lights,
fearing a collision
that would catapult father's corpse
into the chill, rainy night air,
a flying body bag and me,
my old man
doing triple somersaults
in the midst of his encroaching rigor mortis,

finally, the embalmer, dazed by the oncoming headlights,
crossed over the median divider,
stopped at the red light,
looked over at me, shrugged, and said,
"Hey, he's at zero-point-place
and nothing else can get at him,
only the great blaze
shines on him now,
he's at homeplate and safe,"
then the light turned green
and my father and the embalmer
drove off into the pure white light of forever.

# BIMBO'S YOUNG SON

Driving my '76 Buick Electra 225
past Tina's house, I see wreaths and lit candles,
facilitating the path for spirits rapidly departing.
A child is running 'round the grieving mother's knees,
the child is hopscotch jumping 'round
lit candles on the sidewalk,
"Don't put them out," the grandmother warns,
while the child talks to the light,
"My daddy, my daddy's there,
in those candles,
in those lights."
Tina grabs her grandchild by the shoulder,
pulls his tiny limbs towards her
and asks, "who told you?
          "Who talked about it?"
The child answers calmly and possessed,
"I see him and that's my dad
and he's dead, look at the lights,
look, you see, he's in there."
I kiss Tina and she asks me,
"How did he know, how did he find out?"
I give no answer,
but invite her to our vigil tonight.

# HIRAM MORALES

The day's light blasting a bouquet
of white, yellow, red flowers
accompany my solo drive to mother in Queens,
trying to remember who they are;
my aunt Carmen, her son now dead,
Ruthie, my cousin, attending my father's last days,
Elba, crying out as she spots her brother Johnny,
Hiram, Jr., grappling with his father's death,
Hersilia, now in college, newly returned home to mourn,
Joshua, Hiram's last son, too young to make it all out,
family, all of them family,
and I knitting with the thinnest thread
of recognition who is who,
what is what,
how he died.
A perfunctory priest solemnly pushes
the commencement prayers on the ailing widow
with pious fast-food-blessings.
Hiram's mother is not yet here
for the incantations to his spirit.
It all ends mysteriously,
tears, shouts, deep guttural,
wrenching, throaty screams,
wounds gaping at the breathless
corpse,          "dejame al ladito de él,
                          al ladito de él,
                          Ay Dios mio,
                          al ladito de él
                          I can't believe it,
                          I can't believe it."
Dante's hell descends sweeter than this,
no molten steel melts flesh

faster than Tia Carmen's breath
wanting to breathe life into Hiram,
      "I can't believe it,
      I can't believe it."
Wailing cries about staying,
      "by your side Hiram,"
your mother's by your side,
and sirens blare from her breast,
      "I can't believe it,
      ay Dios mio,
      I can't believe it."
Death's impatient hand grips hard,
steady, compelling Hiram's soul
to part,
to move away from flesh,
Tia Carmen can't believe it,
not her Hiram, not her boy,
      "I can't believe it,
      Socorro dejame al ladito de él,
      al ladito de él,
      I can't believe it."

# YEYA

## I. Mitchel

Cuando niño a mi
siempre me preocupaban
las conversaciones adultas,
especialmente las de Tía Yeya
y Tío Gumito,
había entre ellos una competencia
llena de amor pero acompañada
con un rigoroso querer saber
el uno más que el otro.
Recuerdo que las monjas
me habían asignado
memorizarme las tablas de multiplicación
les doy un ejemplo:
    2 por 2 son 4
    6 por 5 son 30
pero cuando yo entraba
en problemas cósmicos
como el 12 x 130
ahí me estancaba
y empezaba a rogarle a Tío Gumito
que me ayudara,
y ese, para mi, era el momento
mágico, porque si Yeya estaba
de visita, ella se las sabía
al pie de la letra,
al segundo ya tenía
mi contestación y mi tarea hecha.
Ahora, si Tío Gumito
también estaba presente
Yeya le preguntaba

"¿Gume, tu que sabes, cuánto es eso?"
Gumito, que nunca se echaba pa'atras
se tiraba de cabeza y ahí empezaban ellos,
como si todavía fuesen niños,
a combatir:
    ¿Cuánto es 5 por 135?
    ¿Cuál es la capital de Egipto?
    ¿Cuántos kilómetros hay de Caguas a Juncos?
Y por ahí seguían.
Para mi era gozoso
porque yo les interponía todas
las preguntas que me asignaban las monjas,
y ya al terminarse mi tarea
me despedía de ellos
y los dejaba en su batalla mental.


    II. Yeya y Nené

Tía Yeya siempre le llamo a papi
Nené,
a mí, cuando niño, me extrañaba un poco,
pero el respeto y el cariño
que Yeya le tenía a mi padre
no era abstracto
sino una cosa táctil,
era un amor concreto,
sólido, hecho de mármol,
y fue ése respeto que Yeya
le tenía a papi
lo que me enseñó
que el respetar de verdad

es el querer, el amar sin temer,
el sentirse uno en la presencia
de una persona noble
donde no hay la posibilidad de la traición,
de la mentira,
donde la negatividad no existe.
Así es como yo entendí
y todavía entiendo
el amor que Yeya le tenía
a su hermano Nené,
y así mismo es que yo,
el hijo de Nené,
quiero a ese hermano que Yeya adoraba.
Aprendí de Yeya a querer
a mi padre con un respeto profundo
y sin temor.


III. Cambucha

Esa mañana me levanté travieso.
Tenía una energía adentro del cuerpo
que no me dejaba quieto.
Corría,
me escondía
debajo de la cama,
me le metía
entre las piernas a Cambucha,
hasta que tropecé con la tabla de planchar
y destrocé la plancha,
que al caerse fundío la electricidad
en la casa entera.

Cambucha, con la paciencia agotada, me castigó,
me amarró con un trapo al pie de la cama,
y me dejó en el cuarto obscuro diciendo
"ahora espero que te calmes."
Lloré, traté de deshacer el nudo,
no pude,
llore más y me dormí
hasta oir la puerta,
cuando Yeya y su hijo,
mi primo Richard, entraron.
De inmediato empecé a llorar y a pedirle
la bendición a Yeya;
tía, tía, tía,
bendición, bendición, bendición,
Yeya me encontró castigado en el cuarto obscuro,
yo me hice el todo pobrecito,
y Yeya me soltó.
Me le escape a Cambucha
por la puerta de la cocina
y al correr hacia el patio
ví lo increible,
mi primo Richard ojeando el palo de mango
con una piedra en la mano,
su ojo puesto sobre el mango
que yo tanto anhelaba.
Habían pasado muchas tardes
durante las cuales yo me saboreaba el mango
que el sol maduraba tan tiernamente.
Pero al regresar, allí
estaba Richard con esa piedra,
listo y con un tino perfecto,
zumbó la piedra,

la cual rozo el mango
y yo que esperaba,
con manos abiertas,
lo cogí y lo sobé,
y me metí debajo de la casa de Doña Wita
para comérmelo.
Richard me sorprendió
y ahí fue que empezó la pelea del mango
Yo la perdí, Richard lo cogió.
Pero de pronto mi primo entendió lo inesperado,
porque Tía Yeya, viendo lo que pasaba,
partió el mango,
mitad para mi y mitad para él.
Mientras ella lo cortaba nos decía
"la familia se lo divide todo"
y me enseñó, en ese momento,
que Richard y yo
tendríamos que gozar
de un eterno compartir.

# YEYA

I. Mitchel

As a child
I was always concerned
about adult conversations,
especially the ones between Aunt Yeya
and Uncle Gumito,
between them
there was a fierce competition
filled with a kind of love
that was accompanied by the strong need of one
to know more than the other.
I remember that the nuns had assigned
for homework the memorization
of the multiplication tables,
for example

    2 times 2 equals 4

    6 times 5 equals 30

but when I encountered
the cosmic problems
such as 12 X 130,
I got stuck
and pleaded to Uncle Gumito for help
and for me that was the magic moment
because if Yeya was visiting
she knew the answer "to the letter"
and in a second
she had my answers and homework completed.
Now, if Uncle Gumito was also present
Yeya would ask him:

"Gume, you who knows, how much is that?"
Gumito, who never gave up,
took on the challenge
and that's when they start their debate,
as if they were still kids:

>How much is 5 times 135?
>What is the capital of Egypt?
>How many kilometers are there between Caguas
>>and Juncos?

and they went on and on.
For me it was fun
because I presented them
with all the questions
assigned by the nuns,
and when my homework was done
I would say good-bye to both
leaving them with their intellectual battle.


II. Yeya y Nené

Aunt Yeya always called dad Nené,
when I was a child I found this
a little bit strange,
but the respect and love
that Aunt Yeya felt for my father
was not an abstract
but a tactile feeling,
a concrete love,
solid, made of marble,
and it was that respect
that Yeya felt for my daddy

that taught me that to respect really means to love,
to love without fear,
to feel the presence of a noble person
where there is no possibility for treason, or lies,
where negative does not exist.
That's how I understood and still understand
the love that Yeya felt for her brother Nené,
and likewise I,
the son of Nené,
love that brother that Yeya cherished.
Through Yeya I learned to love my father
with a profound respect
and without fear.


### III. Cambucha

That morning I woke up naughty
inside me I had the kind of energy
that did not let me stay still.
I ran,
hid under the bed,
romped through Cambucha's legs
until I knocked against the ironing table
and destroyed the iron
which on its way down
caused an electrical shortage in the house.
Cambucha, whose patience was exhausted, punished me,
tied me with a rag to the foot of the bed,
left me in a dark room.
I cried, tried to undo the knot,
but couldn't.

I cried some more and fell asleep in the dark bedroom
until I heard the door opening
and Yeya and her son, my cousin Richard,
came in.
Immediately I began to cry
and to ask for Yeya's blessings;
auntie, auntie, auntie,
bless me, bless me, bless me.
Yeya found me punished in the dark room,
all withered and pained.
She untied me.
I escaped from Cambucha
through the kitchen door
and ran to the backyard,
there was my cousin Richard with his eye
on the mango tree,
a rock in his hand,
aiming at the mango that
I desired so badly.
For many afternoons
I had savored that mango
that the sun was tenderly ripening.
With perfect aim Richard
threw the rock,
I waited for the mango with my hands wide open.
I caught it and caressed it
and went under Doña Wita's home
to eat it.
Richard followed me
and that's when the fight started.
I lost, Richard got the mango.
Yeya, now aware of the situation,

took the mango and cut it
half for me
and half for him.
As she was cutting it she told us
"the family shares everything,"
and at that moment
I learned that Richard and I
would have to enjoy an eternal sharing.

Translation by Sandra A. García

# HILLEBRAND FUNERAL PARLOR, WOODHAVEN BOULEVARD

Some mourners bear their pain behind delicate smiles,
others irrigate their loss
with voluminous cataracts of tears.
But my father's family arrived carrying
brown paper bags filled with memories,
vodka, cranberry juice,
and other losing preparations
that shorten life and lengthen pain.

We probably should've stayed
in the Bronx,
but mother preferred
"a more classical environment"
for father's farewell,
a kind of upscale, white stucco walls,
Hollywood cornices, wall to wall
acrylic parlor.

Yet heart to heart feelings
fill the Naugahyde vinyl room
that could have made father's
death a plastic jubilee.

Father was simple, clean,
transparent, irrepressibly patient,
no absence of humility or love
in him,
he was blessed at birth
and during his stay he shared
a life of love, no surprises, even in his death
there were no surprises.

He lived as cleanly as he loved.
Father may you enter
the kingdom of clean, clear,
unfettered living,
may a pure trumpet tone announce
your entrance into translucent space.

# MICHAEL SKOLNICK

I.

Time past, time present,
time future, you and I,
we used to, in time past,
count syllables, check on end-rhymes,
diagnose language directed to body/listener,
chemical exposure to grammar,
nothing, no thing,
like two men telling stories
in rhymed verse to each other.
Michael, in time past,
we were joined at the ear
and shared a common blood flow,
now, suddenly, you are time future,
damn how could I have known
I'd be time present,
you time past and future,
Michael, you better start whispering
the whereabouts of the spirits
from your vantage point.
They have got to be playing numbers
and hovering over Adela's restaurant on Avenue C
waiting for closing time
to collect leftover food
for homeless Angels residing in Tompkins Square Park.
Oh Michael remember how we read
*Hamlet* and *The Merchant of Venice,*
together in time present,
but now, you're past and future in one
and I'm left out,
alone, once more.

II.

How could I have known
that I'd arrive early at
Riverside-Gramercy Chapels,
how could I have known the aggression
of the chapel attendant,
       "You're early, too early,"
how could I have known you're to be seen at six
and that I'd get there at five,
how could I have known I'd be late for your
earliness,
that your name thundering in my ears
would be Gabriel's trumpet
announcing to the world
that you now counsel the Lord,
Yahweh, that He is now getting
some of the best advice Heaven can get,
how could I have known
that Bob Rosenthal would be in tears,
when I telephoned for your number,
years had passed, seasons had gone and come
but your name thundered in my mind
Monday night.
Tuesday morning, from my office,
where you and I used to talk
about literature, Richie, Marilyn,
Kathy, and my Siamese cats,
Tuesday, I called you because you rained
upon me like a monsoon of memories,
Tuesday, when I called for you Bob wept,
and well, Michael, how could I have known.

# ALVIN ASCENDS

When the procession has arrived,
I will sing to you,
the choir will sing to you,
the angels will do double arabesques
and all the sky will sparkle
with hands and feet stretched
to touch your departing mantle.
Max Roach will play vibrant dark drum rolls
as the procession moves its funereal beat
slowly,
very slowly,
Arthur Mitchell, Tally Beatty,
George Faison, Gary de Loatch,
Keith McDaniels, Marilyn, Mari,
all moving slowly,
Roach playing los palitos,
composed, denying overt tears,
Butler, Premice,
Mrs. Cooper held,
Chenault Spence lighting Alvin's path,
designing at this very moment
a yellow, white road for the Master's next move,
Judith Jamison more striking and balanced than ever,
David Dinkins poised to lead New York
in an invitation to the Lord to lift our Alvin,
on high, for his is the resurrection,
        the life,
and as Alvin believed,
and as Alvin's eyes beheld Him,
and as he created for Him,
Alvin shall never die.
With nothing he came,

with no thing he leaves,
he saw our holy world
revealed through gospel music,
he reworked and made old things new,
"it is done my Lord, and now I am your son,"
said Alvin, as he twisted torsos
into a praising of the Lord, begging Him to
  fix me, Jesus, fix me,
  fix me for my errant ways,
  fix me, Jesus, fix me,
  for I've Been 'Buked and Scorned
  and talked about from shore to shore,
  so fix me, Jesus, fix me,
  and as you know that day by day,
  by legions we all die Lord,
  and since you know, O Lord,
  that We've Been 'Buked and Scorned
  fix us, Jesus, fix us
and Jesus does fix,
Jesus fixes when Ashford and Simpson
sing good-bye to you Alvin,
Jesus fixes when Judith exhorts
Alvin as her spiritual leader
who made her believe that she could fly,
  that she could cry,
  and by the time
  that she had danced his cry
Alvin would ask her "What now?"
After the bravos, the screaming adulation,
the hollering audience, after the triumph
she'd find that Alvin had already moved
  to that empty space

where Judith would have to travel again
        with her spiritual walker,
knowing she would have to cry anew
not because she would die
but because she would be born again
        in another dance,
yielding up the secrets of her heart to him,
again, over, again, over, again.
Alvin will not shut his eyes and ears
O Lord, immortal Creator and Maker of Man,
give rest, O Christ, to your Servant Alvin,
let him go down to dust
where sorrow and pain are no more,
where the days and nights are past and gone, O Lord,
        rocka-his-soul in the bosom of Abraham,
        rocka-his-soul in the bosom of Abraham,
        rocka-his-soul in the bosom of Abraham,
and let him remain with you for all time,
listen, Lord, to Roberta Flack loving Alvin always,
listen, Lord, to Max Roach,
listen to Max for his drums are the last pulse
before Alvin's ascension,
listen, O Lord, to how the cymbals announce
his arrival at your house,
listen to his simple knock,
no fanfare, just a worker Lord,
a suppliant choreographer knocking at your door.

# MICHAEL ST. CLAIR

So as we drove
south on the FDR Drive,
both of us drunk,
you risked it,
you hit my face
as I drove,
shocked I said,
"do it again and I'll
drive you into the wall."
I loved you,
I created my very first ballet
on your body,
remember how I drove you,
"Miguel this piece of music
lasts twenty minutes,
your steps and balances
are intricate and I can't
keep it up,
I need to breathe,
just a second's worth
of oxygen,
you hear me?"
No, I didn't,
I wanted that well-tuned
instrument of yours to play
restlessly,
no stand still catch breath
break for you.
I remember Alvin watching us
struggle to make music visible,
Ailey chided me,
"He can't go on like that,

he's got to breathe."
No, I said,
"He's got to dance to music
till we both collapse."
And faint we did,
you from lack of oxygen
and I from spent inspiration,
the work, the trips to Oberlin,
the unfinished ballet,
the angry yelling,
"why did you stop, Michael
why did you do that to me?"
Now I know it wasn't me,
you made a call
a time is up decision,
and I was squealing,
like a pig at a slaughtering,
yet I knew we'd make it,
but now you're transparent
escaping through the hole
in the ozone layer,
move on, Michael,
I'll catch up to you,
we'll dance again.

# LUCKY CIENFUEGOS

### (The Man of a Hundred Fires)

#### I. Lucky Talks

Don't cry when I die,
it's not pain, it's a setting forth,
no tears can wash away my smell,
so forget the liquid rush,
and get some words to say
how I held time in my veins,
pulsating, digressing, begetting,
regretting, embedding
noun–verb–object
relationships into my coffin,
don't cry, just tie a knot
of words whereby I won't forget
you still remember.


#### II. Lucky's Presence

No sectioned, spliced genetic slide
can tell how he smoked, walked, gulped,
talked 'bout women 'tween their thighs,
expert he,
      on how they slid towards
his ultimate instrument of intrusion,
that which penetrates all ego,
leaving fuming, moistened dreams
of mucous film on blood-stretched skin
made hard by male desire.

### III. The Fires Are Extinguished

So what if you're dead,
I'm here, you're gone,
and I'm left alone
to watch how time betrays,
and we die slow
    so very slow,
we talked of sharing time
beyond quadruple-heart-bypass
and non-clotting-blood
that spills like your last breath forever,
without stoppage,
no heart-beat in you my friend,
no pulse, I fear I'm all alone.

# ON SEEING MIKY'S BODY

### (7th Street and Avenue A)

What the hell are you
doing in there?
Your lips sewn,
your eyelids shut
       for
         ever.
What do you think you're doing
hidden in that casket?
Come out, come on out
and let's play,
what's a guy to do
without you, without CienFuegos,
without his main mellow men?
Who's a guy to play with?
Make words with.
Got to get you back!
How come you let me go,
didn't I love you
with the right "e"?
Not the one for empty,
not the one for enough,
but the one for eternally,
like I'm eternally yours,
you eternally mine,
but now, now you can't
come play with me
in Tompkins Square Park,
and I can't get mad at you?
Figure that one out!
Who am I going to be mad at?
Damn you take a lot of liberties

leaving me in Loisaida
with all my planets atwirl,
silly like a spinning child,
swirling and straining,
and crying too,
like the day I was chasing you
in Tompkins Square Park
to make you stop saying
what you were saying about me,
I don't remember now
what it was you were saying,
but I skinned my knee
trying to catch up to you
and what would I have done
had I caught up to you
except shake you and hug you
and jump into our usual jump-rope,
just you, me, and Lucky skipping,
twirling the rope faster and faster
till we could shout at him
you're out,
at which point Lucky would say,
"it beez that way sometimes
and even after I die,
it'll be that way always."

# Afterword

*Things of August: The Vulgate of Experience*
by Roy Skodnick

Miguel Algarín's *Love Is Hard Work* reads like an almanac, with the grave stinging authority of Hesiod's *Works and Days*. The figures of sowing, cultivating, harvesting and burying in the seasonal rhythm of the earth's turning gather fatal resonance and power in this record of lives and deaths of "sacred" friends and members of the poet's family. Private loves and public collaborations are celebrated and mourned, and the poet doesn't spare himself: his own infirmity becomes the scalding center of his book, which is carefully constructed with formal "Proems" that open each of the four sections. Algarín has found a classical form: the great agricultural year of the world's body structures the slow accumulating force of his book's hard work. The sights, sounds and smells of the daily round provide the compost and manure for his heroic work. Like Whitman, Algarín is a sentinel of the city's streets. He listens to "the blab of the pave," and is a nosy observer of all its teeming, often dangerous life, on whom no swift fleeting mortal beauty is lost. Like William Carlos Williams, he constructs his poetic line from the human buzz, the exclamatory radiance of people coming together. The poet as healer, provider of care and consolation, attaches him to Williams's student Allen Ginsberg, another longtime denizen of the Lower East Side, whose poetry makes community. Like Paul Goodman, Algarín practices a literary nurturing that builds and preserves cities, castigates and defeats enemies, in order to sustain Polis, in the august formal sense of the Greek word. Charles Olson's definition "polis is / eyes" and "there are only / eyes in all heads, / to be looked out of" bears kindred weight. Algarín works in this American poetic tradition, which assumes concrete ethical responsibility.

Not only Miguel's poetry puts him in such company, but the explosive cultural force of the institution he created on Loisaida, with several of the friends and lovers catalogued here. Four of the most important now are gone (Miguel Piñero, Lucky CienFuegos, Bimbo Rivas and Richard August). Others who created in the orbit of the Nuyorican Poets Cafe—Michael Skolnick, Michael St. Clair and Alvin Ailey—are given moving elegies. The associated figures of dances performed, music played and dramas created accumulate throughout the book. Behind these poems are two other masters of civilizing civic grace, whom Algarín has celebrated elsewhere, George Balanchine and Joseph Papp. The cafe as a thriving pioneer institution has deep roots in Papp's Public Theater, where Algarín and Piñero worked. It is no exaggeration to place Miguel next to these two supreme New York City artist-impresarios, whose every moment was calibrated to the turbulence and excitement of the city. From its cacophony, racial tension and continual renewal are born resilient secular art forms. These poems, like scores and scripts, put New York into motion.

Algarín has been "On Call" (the title of another book) for a quarter century now, since he moved back to the neighborhood where he grew up. In the seventies, his long, narrow ground-floor apartment at 524 East 6th Street, the site of many poems, was the center of a neighborhood movement that organized the New York Latino community through poetry, drama, dance and music. By training and education, Algarín was well prepared to lead it. I met him when we were graduate students at Rutgers, where Miguel was already a popular teacher and an exotic, erudite student of comparative literature. He was leading a furiously complex private life, which included multiple love affairs, orchestrated by his passionate interests in dance, philosophy and poetry. He was writing his Ph.D. thesis on Immanuel Kant and Wallace Stevens, but he eventually earned his degree by translating Pablo Neruda's poems on

Puerto Rico, a sign of his more engaged public career. That Algarín was ready to instigate symbolic events in culture was announced by asking Neruda to read one of his anticolonial Puerto Rican poems at Columbia University. Neruda, no stranger to political rhetoric, protested that he didn't have a copy. His translator quickly provided it. Miguel was always an effective provocateur, reminding even the committed of their continual obligations to be "On Call." I was standing next to him when he met Allen Ginsberg, at that moment in a cast for a broken leg. Algarín, speaking in rapid street Spanish, which Ginsberg gamely accepted, challenged him on some point of community vigilance. His unrelenting linguistic assault resulted in Ginsberg's lunging out to kick him, cast and all: An important friendship was born. My interest in the Black Mountain Poets at the time provided Miguel with the confirmation of his own projective line. We listened "goggle-eared" to a tape of Charles Olson's no-holds-barred Berkeley reading of 1965, and Miguel found exuberant support for what he already knew: As Olson says, "Poetry is dancing sitting down." He was then putting together his first book (still unpublished), *Agon,* inspired by Balanchine's choreography, lovingly notated and typed by Richard August, with whom he was living, and with whom he made the move to the Lower East Side. Richard August's presence in the early years of the cafe was crucial. In the third section of this book, "August in Loisaida," the pun of Richard's name is elaborated day by day, as Miguel records the moment of their breakup, in the context of all their works and days, living the hectic lives of local cultural leaders. Bittersweet, but sweet nonetheless, the making of peach jam is a metaphor writ large for all the binding fluids that connect life to life. Another essential participant in the life of the cafe, Lois Elaine Griffith, makes her appearance, and the tender incidental goings and comings of neighborhood punctuate the eruption of clamor and crisis.

Stevens and Kant: An ambitious coupling of sensuous vision with rigorous moral and aesthetic philosophy was an index of Miguel's singular presence in those bygone "pastoral" university years, when Vietnam-Cambodia protests and Black Power politics set the pace on the Livingston College campus. He was his own best example of his first poem here, "Nuyorican Angel": It was a new experience to sense his "Lines of fluid fire" and how "his eyes [could] penetrate emotional lead." He began "kicking the mind apart" the first moment I met him at a faculty party, the young black-haired slim-waisted Miguel with the glistening mustache, shining teeth and bright angel's eyes. He did "[scorch] living flesh," and this Latino graduate student had already developed a complete philosophy of vision in his passionate attention to poetry. He could logically quote Stevens's words: "I am a native in this world / And think in it as a native thinks." Vision was rife in those days, but Miguel's was immediate and precise. Few graduate students took up such a visionary challenge. Those who did, Jim Ruddy (the subject of yet another elegy), Marilyn Kallet, Kathy Stein, Michael Skolnick, myself and a growing band of his own students, found in Miguel's beauty of body and speech a burning attention that left the academy behind and initiated a kind of friendship that changed one's life. The fidelity he offered was unique. Not love's fidelity in the strict sense (his worldly imperatives were too complex for that), but a lover in the mind, our best witness to all that could transpire in a flash. One more poetic presence must be added to the list above, that of Robert Duncan, whose gargantuan sensual and intellectual curiosity took great pleasure in Miguel's presence. Duncan's description of how "the poet's voice, the whole beauty of the man Olson" lifts us up "to where the disturbance is, where the words / awaken / sensory chains between being and being" applies to both himself and Algarín. Such poetic strength and majesty were to bear fruit in Miguel's public career. In these early years, he was preparing. Those of us included in his private life were not surprised when he assumed the mantle. Like Amiri Baraka, another close companion whose poetry made him shoulder the leadership of his community, Miguel never looked back. He continues to teach at Rutgers, however, where his Shakespeare course still astounds students, informed as it is by the dynamic theatrical life bound up in the cafe's proven performance aesthetic.

Stevens provides penetrating glosses for this book. The acceleration that illness imposes on the poet puts him "On the threshold of heaven" where "the figures in the street / Become the figures of heaven." Thus the angels of the first part. But the quake and tumult of this poetry are quite original: "The backdraft caused by the Angel's wing" delivers news that "this city will not be bombed." The flatline of loved ones already gone is relieved only by "The Passing On of Tradition" when the supreme artistry of Savion Glover and Gregory Hines floods the cafe. Nevertheless, the poet, the prosaic Mitch as he jocularly dubs himself, continues to explore neighborhood, bedroom and funeral parlor, very much like Whitman in his work as "The Wound Dresser." The rigor is exacting. After checking himself out "cara a cara," "Mitch sees all except himself": Instead, a reproduction of "Van Gogh / *Sunflowers*" in a mirror bursts into flame. There are visitations of Angels, of course, sometimes beautiful, sometimes obese: The poems unfold their spiritual discipline amid old joys and new temptations. As Stevens wrote, "The total grandeur of a total edifice" appears through the cracks in the sidewalk, and a "Nuyorican Angel Voice" swells into a master's summary of the art of the perfect musical phrase. Or the earth's new electronic skin of telecommunication, "Lower East Side English radio-speak / sounds like Mayan to the Japanese," is celebrated with yet another old friend from Rutgers, Akira Nogami, who brought Miguel's poetry to Japan. The peril of the streets always intrudes, and Miguel's witness is aided by the momentary appearances of old allies, like Miguel Piñero, "Angel of Records": Sagelike recollections of daily events become parables for continued use. Only someone really knowledgeable of the world's pleasures could provide such a moving example of ascetic discipline: "I don't want to busy my desires." The sudden pause to elaborate a total aesthetic "Note for a Poet" is no surprise. But "Nuyorican Angel Hypericin" breaks altogether new ground, as it documents the experience of being an experimental animal. The old life of "The Bi-Sexual Super Macho" pulls him back into the streets he is such a master of, and the extremes of criminal behavior in "Serial Killer Angel" must also be explored. The poet studies the great world of present strife: Meditations on history on the Lower East Side, a defense of the cafe itself by Piñero's achieved historical voice as "our cultural DNA"; Mitch wandering the unsettling streets of Berlin, after the Wall has fallen, to the site of the synagogue where Kristallnacht began, where new kinds of ethnic violence in old Europe threaten; and the specter of universal hunger in

Africa with the anticlimactic appearance of the American army witnessed only by the world's media—these are the three huge culminating poems of the first part, which set the stage for Algarín's "Bio/Ethics in an Age of Plagues." Algarín takes his condition as something of a gruesome, sometimes comic riddle: how to live with the disease. Present lifesaving imperatives are his subject, but ingenious solutions are explored as well, punctuated always by remembrance of past loves and the continual "bio-chemical depression" he suffers when "the song of the river forgot him."

The third section is the center of the book, the active search for times past in order to be equal and faithful to the recalcitrant present, the almanac-construction of deep being that Loisaida is for Miguel Algarín. I've walked those streets for years with him, illuminated by his step-by-step recollection of the lineaments of forgotten people and buildings. We overhear the poet-in-the-making absorbing the complex genealogies of neighborhood. The unhitched horses, the shared blintzes, the bittersweet complexity of broken love. The inheritor of Williams finds life still unabashed and burgeoning. In the backyards, the natural world stirs. The leading action of the poet himself, even in the face of death, is "clearing the impulses of the breath / for each step the dancer takes." In this section we draw closest to his intimate world, his gallivanting adventures with companions, even a berserk bus chasing the poet's van. Occasionally I accompanied the three poets Miguel, Miky and Lucky in their charismatic dashes through neighborhood and city, absorbing their quick inflections of bilingual speech, as they honed a shared poetic mind. Whole language fields, every cadenced nuance, stopped on a dime. Intonation was sharpened like a fine blade. They were supremely conscious of what they were accomplishing: Their exuberant perceptions were tagged and grooved for further use, litanies of poems would be recited like charms and taunts against intruders. Demons were stopped in their tracks. Storming their urban heaven, they unloosed comic thunder in the street. The apartment on Sixth Street was home for a motley assembly of passers-through. Signal and beat of the neighborhood scratched at the window and collided through the door. "Oye, Miguel!"—this galvanizing shout in the street, incessant claim of the neighborhood's awakening confidence in their own culture, street lives in action for Loisaida.

The insistent meditation on lost love seeps through in the major movement of the poetry, "the anger-glow of severed love." "August 12" registers the agonizing moment of breakup. Broken glass is the terrifying noise that reverberates through the series. The poet's summer season with its lush fruits will always pun with lost love, the name of August. Sister Irma's ministering care, interludes of homecoming with Maria to Puerto Rico, a Chekov play translated into Latino inflections in Brooklyn, these are the swarming celebrations of urban life's richness, and the ripening peaches on the trees in the yard. The insistent sweet imperative of blooming summer, despite the echo of broken glass, recriminations and immediate crises in the neighborhood, like Lina being raped, reign in the poet's mind. He ends in front of the great neighborhood Church of St. Mark's where poetry has always flourished. The Whitman poet records another necessary moment of poetic responsibility, cleaning up the beshitted shorts of a neighborhood kid.

The fourth section, "Nuyorican Kaddish," moves back to formal grandeur, invokes the challenge to "forGet" all the great gone names of historic Latino culture and then concentrates on the death of the poet's father, "A Daniel, a Solomon" of sweet ordinary justice in the home. The poet records all the details of physical ministering and grief, the slow passage to flatline, even the final comic and absurd voyage of his father's body driven the wrong way up Queens Boulevard to the funeral parlor. The reader is plunged into the deepest reserves of the poet's early experience, the almost claustrophobic love of a Puerto Rican family, aunts and uncles, local examples of struggle and rectitude: the tragic enigma of family life. Alvin Ailey receives the big cathedral elegy that he deserves, with all the great dancers and musicians in attendance, but the book ends more intimately with elegies for Lucky and Miky. For Lucky, no easy sentiment, no tears for the clear-eyed streetfighter who demanded "Don't cry when I die." I happened to be with Miguel when he got the news that Lucky had passed. He struggled to contain his tears, as he began to write. But just as he had followed Piñero's instructions to scatter his ashes on the Lower East Side, he remained true to this friend's injunction. Lucky exemplified the stoic discipline of looking at death unvarnished. He was the poet who electrified the city with the greatest performance poem ever. Anyone who heard Lucky—a Hebraic angel of vengeance and justice—dance, curse and sing the lines "Rockefeller, Rockefeller / Genocide, Genocide" in his great poem "Attica" knows why Miguel hears him say now "I held time in my veins / pulsating, digressing, begetting . . . / noun-verb-object / relationships into my coffin." Finally, he ends with the affectionate, low-key, intimate and furtive address to his mighty equal, Miguel Piñero, whose body appears to him. We have a momentary vision of the immortal triad, who gave birth to the living ecstasy of Loisaida:

> *and what would I have done*
> *had I caught up to you*
> *except shake you and hug you*
> *and jump into our usual jump-rope,*
> *just you, me, and Lucky skipping,*
> *twirling the rope faster and faster*
> *till we could shout at him*
> *you're out*

To which Lucky, the mordant sardonic joker, who sees life and death whole without a blink, adds:

> *"it beez that way sometimes*
> *and even after I die,*
> *it'll be that way always."*

Recent history. These are the words and deeds of poets. The Habla of Loisaida.

# Index of First Lines

CPSIA information can be obtained at www.ICGtesting.com
Printed in the USA
LVOW07s2152030414

380285LV00001B/193/A